T

GROSSEST

BOOK
OF
WORLD
RECORDS

By
Mel Cebulash

Illustrated by Darryle Purcell

A TRUMPET CLUB SPECIAL EDITION

Published by The Trumpet Club
1540 Broadway, New York, New York 10036

ISBN 0-440-83029-X

This edition published by arrangement with Writers House Inc.

Illustrated by Darryle Purcell
Printed in the United States of America
Originally published under the title *The Grossest Book of World Records #2*

April 1993
1 3 5 7 9 10 8 6 4 2
OPM

For
My Brother Ira

ADULT BODY
(BALDEST)

BEN SMITH OF LEXINGTON, KENTUCKY, HOLDS THE RECORD. AFTER ONE MONTH (SEPTEMBER 1990), OUR INVESTIGATORS FOUND ONLY **TWO HAIRS** (RIGHT NOSTRIL) GROWING ON BEN'S ENTIRE BODY. "I'VE BEEN BALD SINCE BIRTH," BEN TOLD US. "ACTUALLY, I DID HAVE ANOTHER HAIR GROWING OUT OF MY LEFT NOSTRIL A FEW YEARS BACK, BUT I THINK IT DIED."

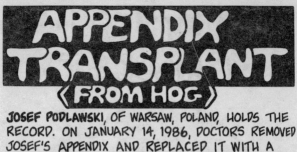

APPENDIX TRANSPLANT ⟨FROM HOG⟩

JOSEF PODLAWSKI, OF WARSAW, POLAND, HOLDS THE RECORD. ON JANUARY 14, 1986, DOCTORS REMOVED JOSEF'S APPENDIX AND REPLACED IT WITH A HOG'S APPENDIX. AS OF JANUARY 14, 1992 (6 YEARS LATER), JOSEF'S TRANSPLANTED APPENDIX WAS FUNCTIONING WELL, AND DOCTORS FOLLOWING HIS PROGRESS EXPRESSED NO CONCERN ABOUT HIS DESIRE TO EAT MEALS OUT OF A SLOP BUCKET.

ARMPIT (SNIFFING)

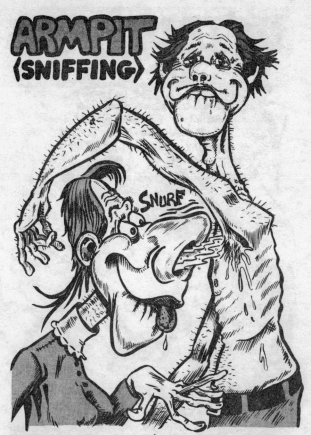

MIRIAM MORTON, OF SOW'S BOTTOM, MINNESOTA, HOLDS THE RECORD. THROUGH SEPTEMBER 8, 1992, MIRIAM HAS SNIFFED THE ARMPITS OF **42,375** PEOPLE. "PEOPLE LINE UP TO LET ME DO IT," MIRIAM TOLD US. "THEY'RE TICKLED AT THE OPPORTUNITY, AND BECAUSE I KEEP LISTS OF THEIR NAMES, THEY KNOW THEY HAVE A SHARE IN THE RECORD."

BEEF HEARTS

(COLLECTION)

HANS KROGER, A RETIRED BUTCHER IN MUNICH, GERMANY, HAS THE WORLD'S LARGEST COLLECTION OF BEEF HEARTS. AS OF MAY 14, 1992, HANS HAD OVER **700** HEARTS IN HIS COLLECTION. HE KEEPS THEM IN A HUGE FREEZER. "ONCE A MONTH, I TAKE THEM OUT AND INSPECT THEM," HANS TOLD OUR INVESTIGATOR. "SOME ARE VERY OLD, BUT THEY'RE VERY FINE. I SUPPOSE THEY'LL BE EATEN AFTER I DIE. I HAVE NO CHILDREN TO CARE FOR THEM."

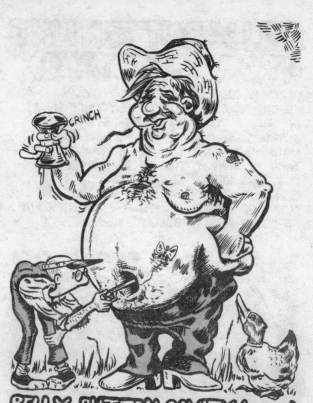

BELLY-BUTTON CAVITY (DEPTH)

GEORGE YOUNG, OF FAT GUT, OKLAHOMA,
HOLDS THE RECORD. IN A TEST HELD ON
MARCH 27, 1984, AN UNSHARPENED PENCIL
WAS INSERTED INTO GEORGE'S BELLY-
BUTTON CAVITY. THE PENCIL REACHED A
DEPTH OF **7 INCHES** BEFORE IT TOUCHED
GEORGE'S BELLY BUTTON. (**NOTE**: WHEN
THE PENCIL WAS WITHDRAWN, IT WAS NOT,
AS SOME NEWSPAPERS HAVE REPORTED,
SHARPENED.)

BELLY-BUTTON LINT (FROM THE STARS)

BARRY BARBER OF LOS ANGELES, HOLDS THE RECORD. BARRY HAS OVER **14 POUNDS** (1992) OF BELLY-BUTTON LINT VACUUMED FROM THE STARS. "I USE A HAND-VAC," BARRY TOLD US. "THE STARS DON'T LIKE TO BE TOUCHED, BUT ASIDE FROM THAT, THEY'RE DARN DECENT PEOPLE. ONE REALLY BIG STAR, AND I'M NOT GOING TO NAME HIM, GIVES ME ABOUT AN OUNCE OF LINT A MONTH FOR NOTHING, AND HE COULD SELL IT, BELIEVE ME."

BOOGERS
(FROM HISTORY)

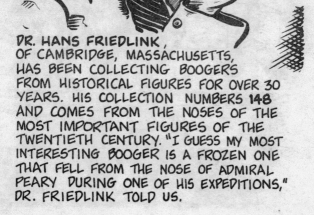

DR. HANS FRIEDLINK,
OF CAMBRIDGE, MASSACHUSETTS,
HAS BEEN COLLECTING BOOGERS
FROM HISTORICAL FIGURES FOR OVER 30
YEARS. HIS COLLECTION NUMBERS **148**
AND COMES FROM THE NOSES OF THE
MOST IMPORTANT FIGURES OF THE
TWENTIETH CENTURY. "I GUESS MY MOST
INTERESTING BOOGER IS A FROZEN ONE
THAT FELL FROM THE NOSE OF ADMIRAL
PEARY DURING ONE OF HIS EXPEDITIONS,"
DR. FRIEDLINK TOLD US.

BOOGER
(HIGHEST PRICED)

A BOOGER AUCTIONED OFF AT A NEW YORK CITY
GALLERY BROUGHT THE RECORD PRICE OF $105,000.
THIS IS, AS FAR AS WE KNOW, THE RECORD PRICE
PAID FOR A BOOGER. IT WAS PRESERVED PER-
FECTLY AND WAS REPUTED TO HAVE COME FROM
THE NOSE OF **CZAR NICHOLAS** OF RUSSIA. (**NOTE:**
THE IDENTITY OF THE BIDDER WAS NOT MADE
PUBLIC.)

AUCTION

BURPING
(GROUP)

THIS RECORD BELONGS TO THE PEOPLE OF GASSUP, NEW MEXICO (POPULATION 752). IN A TAPED SESSION ON JANUARY 14, 1992, THE PEOPLE OF GASSUP RECORDED AN UN-BROKEN BURPING NOISE THAT LASTED FOR **14 HOURS AND 39 MINUTES**. (NOTE: THE TAPE WAS PLAYED INTO THE CONGRESSIONAL RECORD ON JANUARY 28, 1992.)

GASSUP N.M.
GROSSEST BOOK O
"BUST"

CALLUS (COLLECTION)

FLORENCE FRANKLIN, OF PEORIA, ILLINOIS, HOLDS THE RECORD. AS OF SEPTEMBER 12, 1992, FLORENCE HAD OVER 200 POUNDS OF CALLUS IN HER COLLECTION. "I SHAVE IT OFF PEOPLE," FLORENCE TOLD US. "THEY DON'T MIND. SOME PEOPLE EVEN AUTOGRAPH THE BIG PIECES."

16

CAT BITES

MAURICE MORRIS, OF NINE LIVES, KENTUCKY, HOLDS THE RECORD. THROUGH 1992, MAURICE HAD BEEN THE VICTIM OF **1,649** CAT BITES. "I'M PROUD OF THIS RECORD BECAUSE I REALLY HAD TO WORK FOR IT," MAURICE TOLD US. "CATS PREFER TO SCRATCH."

CAT TEETH
(COLLECTION)

MARGIE NORMAN, OF NEWARK, NEW JERSEY, HOLDS THE RECORD. THROUGH 1992, MARGIE'S COLLECTION OF CAT TEETH NUMBERED 5,139. "I USED TO BUY THEM," MARGIE TOLD US, "BUT LATELY MANY WONDERFUL PEOPLE HAVE BEEN SENDING THEM TO ME. THEY KNOW I'LL TAKE GOOD CARE OF THE TEETH. I LOVE EVERY TOOTH IN MY COLLECTION."

CATERPILLAR EATING (LIVE)

WALTER LUCAS OF DENVER HOLDS THE RECORD. IN A CONTEST HELD ON LABOR DAY, 1989, WALTER ATE 17 LIVE CATERPILLARS IN **22 MINUTES**. THE 17TH, A GREEN ONE, BROKE A TIE AND GAVE WALTER THE RECORD. "MY PLAN WAS TO SWALLOW THEM WHOLE," WALTER TOLD US, "BUT I HAD A SORE THROAT. SO I CHEWED THEM. I WAS REAL PLEASED THAT I COULD DO IT." SO ARE WE, WALTER!

CB RADIO
(GROSSEST HANDLE)

AS FAR AS WE CAN TELL, **JESSE WALLACE** OF MOBILE, ALABAMA, DESERVES THIS RECORD. JESSE'S HANDLE IS **BIG PUKE FROM MOBILE.** "I TRAVEL AROUND AND TALK TO A LOT OF PEOPLE," JESSE TOLD US, "BUT NO ONE EVER ANSWERS ME. I'M GETTING A BETTER SEND-ING UNIT, AND IF THAT DOESN'T WORK, I'M GETTING A NEW HANDLE." SOUNDS LIKE THE UNIT, JESSE, SO KEEP CALLING!

CIGAR BUTTS
(COLLECTION)

LARRY LINCOLN, OF TAMPA, FLORIDA, HOLDS
THE RECORD. AS OF JANUARY 14, 1992, LARRY'S
COLLECTION OF CIGAR BUTTS NUMBERED 23,345.
LARRY, 72, HAS BEEN COLLECTING BUTTS FOR
60 YEARS. "I REFUSE DONATIONS," LARRY
TOLD US. "I'VE DEVOTED MY WHOLE LIFE TO
COLLECTING CIGAR BUTTS, AND I DON'T NEED
ANY HELP AT THIS STAGE."

CLAPPING (GROUP)

THE PEOPLE OF **BIG HAND**, VIRGINIA, HOLD THE RECORD. AS OF APRIL 1992, THERE HAS BEEN A RESIDENT OF BIG HAND CLAPPING IN THE TOWN'S SQUARE EVERY MINUTE OF EVERY HOUR OF EVERY DAY SINCE APRIL 1942 (**50 YEARS**). "WE WELCOME NEWCOMERS," THE MAYOR OF BIG HAND TOLD US, "BUT THOSE WHO DON'T WANT TO SHARE IN THE CLAPPING SHOULD MOVE ELSEWHERE. WE BELIEVE IN WORKING TOGETHER." AND ANYONE WHO MOVES THERE DESERVES A BIG HAND!

SLURP

COBWEB (EATING)

ROBERT ARMSTRONG OF GREENWICH, CONNECTICUT, HOLDS THE RECORD. IN A CONTEST HELD ON MAY 3, 1983, ROBERT ATE **742** COBWEBS IN LESS THAN FIVE MINUTES. "I TRAINED FOR THE RECORD," ROBERT TOLD US, "BUT I NEVER WOULD HAVE GUESSED I COULD EAT THAT MANY COBWEBS. THEY TASTE BETTER THAN MOST PEOPLE THINK."

DANDRUFF
(EATING)

FOR CENTURIES, THE PEOPLE OF **GOTSHAIR**, A
SMALL ISLAND IN THE ATLANTIC, HAVE THRIVED
ON A DIET (PARTIAL) OF DANDRUFF. THEY HAVE
THE RECORD BECAUSE THEY ARE THE ONLY OPEN
DANDRUFF EATERS. (REPORTS OF CLOSET DAN-
DRUFF EATERS HAVE NEVER BEEN SUBSTANTIATED.)
IN 1984 A DANDRUFF DROUGHT THREATENED THE
HEALTH OF THE PEOPLE OF **GOTSHAIR**, BUT DO-
NATIONS FROM THE PEOPLE OF TEGRIN, NEW
JERSEY, EASED THE PROBLEM UNTIL THE
DROUGHT ENDED.

DEAD ANIMAL IDENTIFICATION ⟨BY SNIFFING⟩

DR. HANS KLEIBER OF VIENNA IS THE WORLD'S GREATEST DEAD ANIMAL IDENTIFIER. IN A TEST ON AUGUST 12, 1985, DR. KLEIBER SUCCESSFULLY IDENTIFIED **43** DEAD ANIMALS BY SNIFFING AT THEIR REMAINS. OF COURSE, DR. KLEIBER WAS BLINDFOLDED DURING THE TEST. "TO BE HONEST," DR. KLEIBER HUMBLY ADMITTED, "I ALMOST MISSED ON THE MUSKRAT. IT SMELLED LIKE A HORSE."

DEAD BATS
(COLLECTION)

DAN BLAKE, OF BLOODSTONE, NEW YORK, HOLDS
THE RECORD. DAN HAD **298** DEAD BATS IN
THE BACK OF HIS DRUGSTORE IN 1991. "I'D
RATHER HAVE LIVE BATS," DAN TOLD US, "BUT
MY CUSTOMERS ARE STRANGE. THEY OBJECT
TO LIVE BATS."

DEAD INSECT (COLLECTION)

PAUL ROACH, OF LADY
PORT, NEW HAMPSHIRE,
HOLDS THE RECORD.
DURING 1987, PAUL'S DEAD
INSECT COLLECTION WENT
OVER THE **ONE MILLION**
MARK. "THAT'S IT FOR
ME," PAUL ANNOUNCED.
"I'VE HAD IT WITH DEAD
INSECTS." (**NOTE**: AN
UNCONFIRMED REPORT
INDICATES THAT PAUL
HAS CHANGED HIS MIND
AND IS COLLECTING AGAIN.)

DIET (HEALTHIEST)

RESIDENTS OF THE SMALL TOWN OF **NATURE'S BEST**, CALIFORNIA, SEEM TO HAVE THE WORLD'S HEALTHIEST DIET. IT CONSISTS OF A DAILY SPOONFUL OF ORGANIC HAIR LICE. (**NOTE:** THE AVERAGE AGE IN NATURE'S BEST IS 97, AND THE OLDEST RESIDENT IS 193.) "WE WANT NEWCOMERS," THE MAYOR OF NATURE'S BEST TOLD US, "BUT WE DISCOURAGE BALD PEOPLE. WE WANT PEOPLE WHO ARE ABLE TO FEED THEMSELVES."

EAR WAX

⟨SCULPTURE⟩

GLENDA RAMBEAU'S, "THE HORSE," A 14-INCH SCULPTURE, IS MADE ENTIRELY OF EAR WAX, AND IS, ACCORDING TO OUR RECORDS, THE ONLY EAR WAX SCULPTURE EVER MADE. GLENDA UNVEILED THE SCULPTURE AT A SHOW IN PARIS IN 1989. "I LIKE WORKING IN EAR WAX," GLENDA TOLD EXCITED SPECTATORS. "IT MAKES YOU FEEL AS IF YOU'RE PART OF THE WORK."

EAR WAX LICKING
(FROM PAY TELEPHONES)

DAN DANNON OF NEW YORK CITY HOLDS THE RECORD. BY HIS OWN COUNT (UNOFFICIAL), DAN HAS LICKED EAR WAX FROM THE RECEIVERS OF MORE THAN **ONE MILLION** PAY PHONES. BY OUR COUNT, DAN LICKED 43,579 RECEIVERS DURING 1991, AND THIS, OF COURSE, WAS SUFFICIENT FOR THE RECORD. TELEPHONE COMPANY OFFICIALS ARE DISTURBED BY DAN'S ACTIONS AND HAVE APPEALED TO FEDERAL AUTHORITIES TO RULE AGAINST RECEIVER LICKING.

EYE GOOK
(COLLECTION)

SANDMAN PHILLIPS, OF BOSTON, HOLDS THE RECORD. AS OF MAY 2, 1992, SANDMAN HAD **47,398** SEPARATE PIECES OF EYE GOOK IN HIS COLLECTION WHICH COMES FROM PEOPLE ALL OVER THE WORLD. "I AM NOW COLLECTING EYE GOOK FROM ANIMALS," SANDMAN INFORMED US. "I GOT INTERESTED AFTER A FRIEND IN SAUDI ARABIA SENT ME SOME CAMEL EYE GOOK. IT WAS REALLY GROSS."

EYE GOOK
(EATING)

MIMI MURINE, 103, OF BARCELONA, SPAIN, HOLDS THE RECORD. EACH MORNING SINCE SHE WAS TEN (**NOTE:** VERIFIED BY LIE DETECTOR TEST), MIMI HAS STARTED HER DAY BY EATING HER EYE GOOK. "I DON'T KNOW IF EYE GOOK HAS HAD ANYTHING TO DO WITH MY LONG LIFE," MIMI TOLD US IN 1990, "BUT I DO KNOW THAT I LOVE THE TASTE OF IT."

FEET
(HAIRIEST)

GEORGE BOYD, OF MONTROSE, CALIFORNIA, HOLDS THE RECORD. GEORGE'S FEET ARE FULLY COVERED WITH HAIR (BROWN) AND HAVE BEEN SINCE HIS BIRTH IN 1950. "I USED TO SHAVE THEM," GEORGE TOLD US, "BUT I GOT TIRED OF STARING AT MY FEET IN THE MIRROR EVERY MORNING. THE ONLY THING I HATE TO DO IS GO SWIMMING IN A POOL. THE LIFEGUARDS ALWAYS TELL ME TO TAKE MY SOCKS OFF."

FEET (SMELL)

ON AUGUST 21, 1991, **WANDA LAKE**, 18, BROKE THE RECORD HELD BY GEORGE DAVID. WANDA REMOVED HER SHOES IN THE CROWDED LOBBY OF A LOS ANGELES THEATER. IN THE FIVE MINUTES THAT FOLLOWED, THE LOBBY WAS A CHAOTIC MASS OF PANIC-STRICKEN PEOPLE TRYING DESPERATELY TO ESCAPE. IN THE END, 42 PEOPLE WERE SICK, AND 14 OTHERS HAD PASSED OUT.

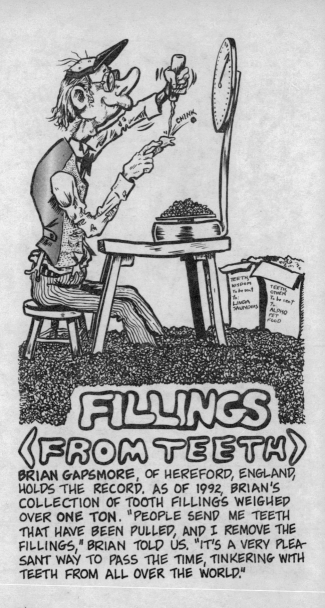

FILLINGS ⟨FROM TEETH⟩

BRIAN GAPSMORE, OF HEREFORD, ENGLAND, HOLDS THE RECORD. AS OF 1992, BRIAN'S COLLECTION OF TOOTH FILLINGS WEIGHED OVER ONE TON. "PEOPLE SEND ME TEETH THAT HAVE BEEN PULLED, AND I REMOVE THE FILLINGS," BRIAN TOLD US. "IT'S A VERY PLEASANT WAY TO PASS THE TIME, TINKERING WITH TEETH FROM ALL OVER THE WORLD."

FROG SKIN (COLLECTION)

BARBARA NEWSOME, OF BLUFFTON, INDIANA, HOLDS THE RECORD. ON MARCH 12, 1991, BARBARA'S COLLECTION OF FROG SKINS NUMBERED 31,742. "I USED TO CATCH THE FROGS MYSELF," BARBARA TOLD US, "BUT NOW I JUST PAY KIDS A NICKEL A SKIN, AND IT GIVES THEM SOMETHING WORTHWHILE TO DO DURING THE SUMMER."

GARBAGE OF ⋆ THE STARS ⋆

JACK KENO, OF LOS ANGELES, HOLDS THE RECORD. EACH DAY SANITATION WORKERS FROM NEARBY BEVERLY HILLS DELIVER GARBAGE COLLECTED FROM MOVIE STARS' HOMES TO JACK'S STORE— THE GAG BAG. "I SELL IT UNOPENED," JACK TOLD US. "YOU'D BE SURPRISED AT HOW MANY PEOPLE WANT GARBAGE FROM THE STARS." JACK USUALLY HAS A TON IN STOCK, AND HE'S ALSO INVESTIGATING WAYS TO SELL GARBAGE THRU THE MAIL.

GARLIC
⟨EATING⟩

JOSEPH VAN DYKE OF PRINCETON, NEW JERSEY, HOLDS THE RECORD. ON JANUARY 14, 1986, JOSEPH CONSUMED 197 CLOVES OF GARLIC IN 42 MINUTES. AFTER THIS EXHIBITION, JOSEPH ATTEMPTED TO THANK PEOPLE WHO HAD APPLAUDED HIS RECORD-BREAKING FEAT, AND SEVERAL OF THEM WERE INJURED IN THE SUBSEQUENT STAMPEDE.

HAIREST LEGS
⟨ADULT⟩

RITA SIMS OF EL PASO, TEXAS, HOLDS THIS RECORD. RITA'S LEGS ARE ENTIRELY COVERED WITH HAIR. **(NOTE:** CHECKED IN 1989.) OTHERS HAVE THE SAME AMOUNT OF HAIR ON THEIR THIGHS AND CALVES, BUT RITA'S FEET, INCLUDING THE BOTTOMS, ARE ALSO COVERED WITH HAIR. "I TRY TO KEEP OFF MY FEET," RITA TOLD US. "I'D HATE TO WEAR THE HAIR OFF AND LOSE THE RECORD."

HAIRIEST LEGS
(CHILD)

THIS RECORD BELONGS TO FRANK ALBERTO OF CULVER, COLORADO. AT AGE TWO (1991), FRANK'S LEGS AND ARMS WERE ENTIRELY COVERED WITH HAIR, EXCEPT FOR BALD PATCHES ON HIS KNEES. "HE'S SO CUTE," FRANK'S MOTHER TOLD US. "HE CRAWLS AROUND THE HOUSE LIKE A LITTLE TEDDY BEAR. I IMAGINE I'LL BE A LITTLE SAD WHEN HE STARTS WALKING." SO WILL YOUR NEIGHBORS.

HEIGHT AND WEIGHT DIVINATION (THROUGH SEAT ANALYSIS)

SUBODH REY, OF NEW DELHI, INDIA, IS THE WORLD'S GREATEST SEAT ANALYZER. DURING A TELEVISED APPEARANCE IN THE U.S., SUBODH CORRECTLY GAVE THE HEIGHT AND WEIGHT OF 20 PERSONS AFTER QUICKLY SNIFFING THE CHAIRS ON WHICH THEY HAD BEEN SEATED. "I CAN'T EXPLAIN IT," SUBODH TOLD US. "IT'S A GIFT."

SLURR

HUMAN LAWNMOWER

PATRICIA LINDEN, OF CHICAGO, ILLINOIS, IS
THE WORLD'S GREATEST GRASS EATER. IN
A TEST HELD ON JULY 4, 1990, PATRICIA
CHEWED UP ALL OF THE INFIELD GRASS
AT CHICAGO'S WRIGLEY FIELD. PEOPLE
WATCHING THIS PRE-GAME TEST GAVE
PATRICIA A STANDING OVATION. "SHE'S
BETTER THAN A LAWNMOWER," ONE
GROUNDSKEEPER TOLD US.

INFESTATION BY MITES (GROUP)

THIS RECORD BELONGS TO THE 3,859 RESIDENTS OF **ITCHY BUTT, MONTANA.** IN 1989, VISITING DOCTORS CERTIFIED THAT EVERY PERSON IN THE TOWN WAS SUFFERING FROM SCABIES, A SKIN DISEASE CAUSED BY MITE INFECTION, "THE MITES SEEMED TO BE JUMPING FROM ONE PERSON TO ANOTHER," THE MAYOR OF ITCHY BUTT TOLD US, "SO WE DECIDED TO GET TOGETHER AND GO FOR THE RECORD."

SMOOCH

KISS OF DOG
(LONGEST)

EVELYN HUNT OF LOS ANGELES HOLDS THE
RECORD. ON NOVEMBER 5, 1986, EVELYN
PLANTED HER LIPS ON JODIE, AN 11-YEAR-
OLD MONGREL, AND HELD THEM ON THE
DOG'S LIPS FOR **SEVEN MINUTES**. EVELYN
WAS DELIGHTED WITH HER RECORD-MAKING
KISS. HOWEVER, JODIE WASN'T AS PLEASED.
AFTER THE ORDEAL, SHE REFUSED TO EAT
AND HAD TO BE TREATED BY AN ANIMAL
PSYCHIATRIST FROM BEVERLY HILLS.

LEFTOVER EATING

LILLIAN BINGAM, 78, CLAIMED THE
RECORD IN 1992. FOR **OVER 50 YEARS**
(NOTE: STILL NOT VERIFIED), LILLIAN
HAS BEEN SLIPPING INTO SEATS IN
CAFETERIAS AND EATING LEFTOVERS.
"I WATCH OUT FOR THIN PEOPLE,"
LILLIAN TOLD US. "THEY NEVER FINISH
THEIR DESSERT."

LEFTOVER POPCORN (COLLECTION)

FRED MORGAN, 17, OF HAMMOND, INDIANA, HOLDS THE RECORD. AS OF JULY 22, 1992, THE TWO-CAR GARAGE BEHIND FRED'S HOME WAS FILLED WITH LEFTOVER POPCORN. TO WARD OFF CHALLENGERS, FRED PLANS TO FLATTEN THE POPCORN AND GIVE HIMSELF MORE SPACE IN THE GARAGE. "I GET MOST OF IT FROM LOCAL MOVIE THEATERS," FRED TOLD US. "MOST PEOPLE DON'T FINISH THEIR POPCORN. I'D HAVE MORE IN MY COLLECTION, BUT SOMETIMES I EAT THE BUTTERED LEFTOVERS. I REALLY LIKE BUTTERED POPCORN."

LIVE SNAIL-SUCKING

ARMAND FORCALQUIER, OF MARSEILLE, FRANCE, HOLDS THE RECORD. IN A CONTEST HELD ON FEBRUARY 12, 1992, ARMAND SUCKED DOWN 1,238 LIVE SNAILS IN A LITTLE OVER 4 HOURS. "IT WAS NOT EASY," ARMAND BOASTED AFTER HE LEARNED THAT THE RECORD WAS HIS. "THEY CLING TO THEIR SHELLS, BUT THEY CAN'T GET AWAY FROM ME."

LONGEST BATH (GROUP)

THE RESIDENTS OF **CULLIGAN**, MONTANA, SHARE THIS RECORD. ON JUNE 14, 1984, ALL 323 OF THEM CLIMBED INTO THEIR BATHTUBS. TWO FULL WEEKS LATER, THEY CLIMBED OUT AND CLAIMED THE RECORD. "IT WASN'T EASY TO LIVE IN A BATHTUB FOR TWO WEEKS," ONE RESIDENT TOLD US, "BUT WE WANTED THE WORLD TO KNOW THAT THE PEOPLE OF **CULLIGAN** AREN'T SOFT."

MILK BONES
(EATING)

IN A CONTEST HELD ON APRIL 26, 1990, LARRY "LASSIE" LINCOLN SET THE RECORD. LARRY ATE 794 MILK BONES IN LESS THAN AN HOUR. LARRY'S CLOSEST COMPETITOR PASSED OUT AFTER EATING 511 MILK BONES AND HAD TO BE TREATED BY A VET, AS THE ATTENDING DOCTOR CLAIMED SHE DIDN'T KNOW THE ANTIDOTE FOR AN OVERDOSE OF MILK BONES.

MUSCLES (FOREARMS)

ARNOLD WEEDNER, 22, HAS THE WORLD'S LARGEST FOREARMS. EACH OF ARNOLDS FORE-ARMS MEASURES **24 INCHES** FLEXED (1991). ARNOLD, WHO WEIGHS 478 POUNDS, TOLD US: "THERE'S NOT AN OUNCE OF FAT ON MY FOREARMS."

MUSCLES (LATS)

JOANNA SHEPHERD, 24, HAS THE WORLD'S BEST DEVELOPED LATS. "I DIDN'T REALIZE THEY WERE SO WELL-DEVELOPED," JOANNA TOLD US, "UNTIL THE DAY I DISCOVERED I COULD FLY." (**NOTE:** JOANNA RECENTLY STARRED IN AERO FILMS' THE BAT LADY OF PARIS.)

MUSCLES
(THIGH)

JUDY BURNS, 19, OF NEW YORK CITY, HAS THE WORLD'S LARGEST THIGH. JUDY'S RIGHT THIGH MEASURES 44 INCHES FLEXED (1990), AND SHE CLAIMS IT'S A RESULT OF BIKE RIDING. "I'M A LITTLE WORRIED ABOUT MY LEFT THIGH," JUDY TOLD US. "IT HASN'T RESPONDED."

NOSE STUFFING
‹LIMBURGER CHEESE›

HANS KLEIBER, OF WEST BERLIN, HOLDS THE
RECORD. IN A CONTEST HELD ON MAY 1, 1986,
HANS MANAGED TO STUFF **13 OUNCES** OF LIM-
BURGER CHEESE INTO HIS NOSTRILS IN LESS
THAN A MINUTE. HANS' CLOSEST COMPETITOR
GAGGED ON NINE OUNCES AND WAS
DISQUALIFIED.

NOSTRIL HAIR
(COLLECTION)

ALICE DRISTON, OF DENVER, HOLDS THE RECORD. AS OF 1992, ALICE'S COLLECTION NUMBERS 11,894 SEPARATE NOSTRIL HAIRS. "NO TWO HAIRS COME FROM THE SAME NOSTRIL," ALICE REPORTED, "BUT I'VE TWEEZED TWO FROM THE SAME NOSE. PEOPLE WHO COOPERATE USUALLY DON'T MIND GIVING TWO."

PERSPIRATION (COLLECTION)

RESIDENTS OF SWEET SWEAT, TEXAS, CAN BE PROUD OF THEMSELVES. USING THE MOTTO "EVERY LITTLE DRIP COUNTS," THEY MANAGED TO COLLECT **42 GALLONS** OF PERSPIRATION DURING THE SUMMER OF 1989. (**NOTE:** OUNCE BOTTLES FROM THE COLLECTION CAN BE PURCHASED FROM THE SWEET SWEAT BOTTLING CO., SWEET SWEAT, TEXAS.)

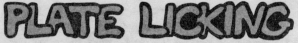

PLATE LICKING

GLORIA EVANS, 62, HOLDS THE RECORD. GLORIA CLAIMS THAT SHE HAS LICKED OVER A MILLION PLATES IN THE FORTY YEARS IN WHICH SHE HAS BEEN LICKING. "IF I GET TO BE FRIENDS WITH THE KITCHEN HELP IN A BIG PLACE, THEY'LL OFTEN LET ME LICK ALL THE PLATES BEFORE THEY WASH THEM," GLORIA TOLD US. "ON A GOOD NIGHT, I COULD GET TO LICK ABOUT 600 PLATES. THAT'S A LOT OF LICKING." IT SURE IS, GLORIA!

POSTAGE STAMPS
(DIET)

HERBERT WINSTEAD, A POSTAL CLERK FROM
TRUE GLUE, KENTUCKY, HOLDS THE RECORD.
TO CONTROL HIS WEIGHT, HERBERT HAS BEEN
EATING POSTAGE STAMPS FOR LUNCH FOR
OVER TEN YEARS. (NOTE: HERBERT'S CO-
WORKERS VERIFIED HIS RECORD.) "BE SURE
YOU MAKE THE POINT THAT THEY'RE CAN-
CELED," HERBERT TOLD US. "I DON'T WANT TO
LOSE MY MEAL TICKET."

PULLING
(WITH GUMS)

CARL HEMBUCK, 82, HOLDS THE RECORD. AT
THE ANNUAL SENIOR CITIZEN'S PICNIC (JULY
4, 1991) IN COLUMBIA, SOUTH CAROLINA,
CARL MANAGED TO PULL A WAGON LOADED
WITH SENIOR CITIZENS (WEIGHING 3,874 POUNDS)
A DISTANCE OF 500 YARDS. CARL MANAGED
THIS AMAZING FEAT WITH THE WAGON HANDLE
HELD BETWEEN HIS GUMS. WE, AT THE GROSSEST,
SALUTE THIS WONDERFUL OLD-TIMER!

RAT TAILS COLLECTION

GLENDA GABOR OF PHILADELPHIA HOLDS THE RECORD. AS OF JUNE 1992, GLENDA HAD **35,432** RAT TAILS IN HER COLLECTION. "I WEAVE THEM TOGETHER," GLENDA TOLD US, "AND MAKE LITTLE RUGS FOR MY APARTMENT. THEY'RE QUITE A SENSATION TO BARE FEET," AND THEY'RE NICE TO LIE ON, TOO, GLENDA!

RAW KIDNEY
(EATING)

ALICE CALDWELL OF BUTTE, MONTANA, HOLDS
THE RECORD. ON OCTOBER 22, 1991, ALICE GOBBLED
UP MORE THAN **14 POUNDS** OF RAW VEAL AND LAMB
KIDNEYS. "KIDNEYS ARE A GOOD SOURCE OF PRO-
TEINS AND VITAMINS," ALICE TOLD US. "IF YOU
COOK THEM, YOU LOSE SOME OF THE VITAMINS.
AS YOU CAN SEE, I DON'T CARE ABOUT THE
RECORD—I CARE ABOUT MY HEALTH."

RAW TONGUE
(EATING)

MIKE McCOY OF COWLICK, TEXAS, HOLDS THE RECORD. ON NOVEMBER 3, 1990, MIKE CONSUMED 7½ POUNDS OF RAW BEEF TONGUE IN 22 MINUTES. "I EAT IT FAST," MIKE TOLD US. "IT TASTES TERRIBLE, BUT I'D DO ANYTHING TO BE ONE OF THE GROSSEST."

ROACH (HIGHEST PRICE)

HOWARD YOUS HOLDS THE RECORD. IN AN AUCTION HELD ON MAY 6, 1991, HOWARD PAID $112,450 FOR LASSIE II, A ONE-YEAR-OLD ROACH OWNED BY SHEILA CIDERMAN OF NEW YORK. "ANYONE WHO KNOWS ANYTHING ABOUT ROACHES KNOWS

THAT THIS ONE COMES FROM CHAMPION STOCK," HOWARD TOLD US. (NOTE: HOWARD DIED A FEW MONTHS AFTER THE AUCTION, AND THE COURT BATTLE FOR CUSTODY OF THE ROACH WAS STILL IN PROGRESS AT THIS WRITING.)

LASSIE II

SOLD

ROACH
(LARGEST)

RITA CARSON, OF PASADENA, CALIFORNIA, CLAIMS THE RECORD FOR HAVING RAISED THE WORLD'S LARGEST ROACH. HER RECORD-SETTING ROACH IS OVER A FOOT LONG AND WEIGHS CLOSE TO **TWO POUNDS** (1992). "PLENTY OF PROTEIN," RITA TOLD US, "AND PLENTY OF GOOD, NATURAL VITAMINS HELPED TO MAKE THIS ROACH INTO A CHAMPION. YOU SHOULD HAVE SEEN IT WHEN I FIRST FOUND IT CRAWLING AROUND MY KITCHEN."

ROACH
(LONGEST LIVING)

LASSIE, A 12-YEAR-OLD ROACH OWNED BY
SHEILA BIDERMAN (1991), IS PROBABLY THE
LONGEST LIVING ROACH IN RECORDED HIS-
TORY. "I'M HONORED TO SEE LASSIE GET IN
THE RECORD BOOK," SHEILA TOLD US. "SHE'S
ALMOST LIKE A MEMBER OF THE FAMILY,
AND IF SHE GETS TOO OLD TO POKE AROUND
THE FOOD BY HERSELF, YOU CAN BET I'LL
DO THE HUMANE THING AND STEP ON HER-
RECORD OR NO RECORD."

HANS GROSCHSCHMIDT, OF HAMBURG, WEST
GERMANY, HOLDS THE RECORD. ON OCTOBER
15, 1991, HANS DOWNED **33 QUARTS** OF SAUER-
KRAUT JUICE IN **45 MINUTES.** ALTHOUGH
HANS WAS RETCHING IN AGONY AFTER HIS
RECORD-SETTING FEAT, HE MANAGED TO TELL
US, "I LOVE SAUERKRAUT JUICE."

67

SNAIL SUCKING
(DEAD)

PIERRE LA TOCHE OF PARIS HOLDS THE RECORD.
IN A CONTEST HELD ON DECEMBER 12, 1991, PIERRE
SUCKED **243** SNAILS OUT OF THEIR SHELLS
IN FIVE MINUTES. "I HAVE BEEN SUCKING SNAILS
SINCE I WAS A LITTLE BOY," PIERRE TOLD US,
"AND EVEN NOW I HATE THE SIGHT OF THE
SLIMY THINGS."

SOCKS
(CONTINUOUS WEAR)

ANDY SCHWARTZ, OF GLEN RIDGE, NEW JERSEY, CLAIMED THE RECORD IN 1989. IN A SWORN STATEMENT, ANDY'S WIFE DECLARED THAT HE HAD WORN THE SAME SOCKS EVERY DAY FOR TWENTY YEARS AND 114 DAYS. IN 1983, SHOE STORES THROUGHOUT NEW JERSEY BANNED ANDY FROM THEIR PREMISES. SINCE THEN HE HAS PURCHASED HIS SHOES THROUGH THE MAIL. ANDY PLANS TO REMOVE THE SOCKS AND TAKE A LOOK AT HIS FEET IN 1999.

SOILED HANDKERCHIEFS

(FROM THE STARS)

LES KNOT, OF LOS ANGELES, CLAIMED THE RECORD IN 1992. LES, 47, HAS BEEN COLLECTING SOILED HANDKERCHIEFS SINCE HE WAS A CHILD. "AT FIRST, I ONLY COLLECTED THEM FROM MY CLASSMATES," LES TOLD US. "THEN ONE DAY A FELLOW IN MY CLASS GAVE ME A DIRTY HANDKERCHIEF THAT HIS FATHER HAD USED. HIS FATHER WAS A STAR IN SILENT MOVIES. FROM THAT DAY ON, I COULD NEVER SETTLE FOR ANY OLD DIRTY HANDKERCHIEF. I'M SURE YOU CAN UNDERSTAND THAT."

SPITTING

(CONTINUOUS)

JESSE JAFFER OF SALVATION, NORTH CAROLINA, HOLDS THE RECORD. IN A CONTEST HELD ON JULY 10, 1991, AT DOWN WIND, PENNSYLVANIA, JESSE MANAGED TO SPIT **10,749** TIMES IN THREE HOURS. "I HOPED TO AVERAGE A SPIT-A-SECOND," JESSE TOLD US, "AND THOUGH I'M A LITTLE DISAPPOINTED, I'M PLEASED TO HAVE THE RECORD." (**NOTE**: JESSE WAS 18 WHEN HE SET THE RECORD, SO HE PROBABLY HAS MANY YEARS OF SPITTING AHEAD OF HIM.)

SPORTS (DEAD RAT THROWING)

DAN MANN, 19, HOLDS THE RECORD. IN A CONTEST HELD ON JULY 4, 1988, IN PASADENA'S ROSE BOWL, DAN HURLED A DEAD RAT (WEIGHING FOUR POUNDS DEADWEIGHT) A DISTANCE OF **312 FEET** FOR THE NEW WORLD'S RECORD. "I HAVE SOME ADVICE FOR YOUNG PEOPLE," DAN TOLD US. "START WITH MICE. A YOUNG ARM ISN'T READY FOR A DEAD RAT."

SPORTS

(FOOT IN MOUTH MARATHON)

PAUL DENNIS OF PALO ALTO, CALIFORNIA, HOLDS THE RECORD. COMPETING IN THE FIRST FOOT IN MOUTH MARATHON HELD IN SAN FRANCISCO ON APRIL 15, 1991, PAUL HOPPED OVER THE 10-MILE COURSE IN EXACTLY 11 HOURS. "MY RUNNING FOOT HELD UP FINE," PAUL TOLD US, "BUT A FEW TIMES I THOUGHT THE OTHER FOOT WAS GOING TO SLIP OUT OF MY MOUTH. I REALLY HAD TO BITE ON IT."

SPORTS
⟨JOGGING WITH DEAD PIGEON IN MOUTH⟩

ON SEPTEMBER 6, 1987, RON DUNCAN OF PHILA-
DELPHIA SET THE RECORD. RON JOGGED A
TOTAL OF **38** MILES WITH THE PIGEON CLENCHED
FIRMLY BETWEEN HIS TEETH. CROWDS LINED
THE ROUTE AND CHEERED RON EVERY STEP
OF THE WAY. "I FELT LIKE ROCKY," RON TOLD
US, "AND I KNEW THIS WAS GOING TO BE
MY DAY."

SPORTS
(MARATHON RUNNING WITH DEAD RAT IN MOUTH)

THIS ANNUAL RACE THROUGH THE STREETS OF CLEVELAND USUALLY HOSTS A LINEUP OF RUNNERS FROM ALL OVER THE WORLD. THE RECORD FOR THE 20-MILE COURSE WAS SET IN 1990 BY MIKLOS KOMETH OF HUNGARY. CARRYING A TWO-POUND RAT BETWEEN HIS TEETH, MIKLOS COVERED THE DISTANCE IN ONE HOUR, 42 MINUTES.

SPORTS

(100 YARD DASH WITH LIVE GOLDFISH IN UNDERWEAR)

PAUL FLETCHER OF LITTLE POND, NEW MEXICO, HOLDS THE RECORD. IN A RACE HELD ON AUGUST 15, 1989, PAUL COVERED THE 100 YARDS IN **10.7 SECONDS**, TOPPING THE OLD RECORD 11.3 SECONDS. THE TOP SPEED OF THE DAY WAS ACTUALLY 10.3 SECONDS, BUT WHEN IT WAS DISCOVERED THAT THE GOLDFISH HAD EXPIRED, THE CONTESTANT WAS DISQUALIFIED.

BOOF

WOOMP

CHICAGO
CITY LIMITS

SPORTS (ROLLING)

PEG PAULLY, OF BALTIMORE, HOLDS THE RECORD. IN 12 DAYS (NOVEMBER 1-13, 1988), PEG ROLLED FROM NEW YORK CITY TO CHICAGO, A DISTANCE OF OVER **700 MILES**. THIS BREAKS THE OLD RECORD OF 493 MILES SET BY MIKE MILTON IN 1971. MIKE WAS ON HAND WHEN PEG ARRIVED IN CHICAGO, AND HIS FRIENDS ROLLED HIM OUT TO GREET HER.

SPORTS (SNOW EATING)

IN 1986, BUFFALO, NEW YORK, HOSTED THIS INTERNATIONAL TEST OF SKILL. CONTESTANTS FROM 24 COUNTRIES LINED UP ON BUFFALO'S MAIN STREET AND WAITED FOR THE SIGNAL TO BEGIN GOBBLING UP THE SNOW THAT COVERED THE THOROUGHFARE. IN THE END, JACQUES PORNIER OF MONTREAL, CANADA, HAD EATEN HIS WAY THROUGH 100 YARDS OF SNOW IN 33 MINUTES. "IT WASN'T DIFFICULT," JACQUES TOLD US, "THE COURSE WAS QUITE FLAKY."

SPORTS (SPITTING-STATIONARY TARGET)

IN A CONTEST HELD AT BARNEY'S KNOCK-EM DOWN AT ATLANTIC CITY, NEW JERSEY, **THERESA "TRENCH MOUTH" VINCENT** SPIT DOWN FOURTEEN CATS (STUFFED) AND WALKED AWAY WITH THE STATIONARY TARGET SPITTING TITLE FOR 1992, QUITE HUMBLE, THERESA TOLD US, "IT TOOK A LOT OF LUCK AND A LOT OF SPIT TO CAPTURE THIS RECORD."

SPORTS
(TOE JAM FLICKING STATIONARY TARGET)

SCORING 5 BULL'S EYES OUT OF 8 FLICKS, JOHN WINSLOW OF LONDON WON THE WORLD'S TOE JAM FLICKING TITLE IN A CONTEST HELD IN CICERO, ILLINOIS, ON APRIL 10, 1986. CONTESTANTS FROM ALL OVER THE WORLD VIED FOR THE TITLE, BUT JOHN WAS AN EASY WINNER. "I DID IT FOR ENGLAND," JOHN TOLD US.

STITCHES
(COLLECTIONS)

FANNY LERNER, OF CATSGUT, ILLINOIS,
HOLDS THE RECORD. AS OF AUGUST 11, 1992,
FANNY'S COLLECTION OF STITCHES WAS 5,389.
"WHEN I WAS A LITTLE GIRL," FANNY EX-
PLAINED, "MY LEG HAD TO BE STITCHED.
LATER, THE DOCTOR REMOVED THE STITCHES
AND LET ME KEEP THEM. THAT GOT ME
STARTED. NOW LOTS OF PEOPLE SEND ME
THEIRS. THEY REALLY HELP KEEP ME IN
STITCHES."

STUFFED RATS
(COLLECTION)

HORACE ODDIE OF NEW YORK CITY HOLDS THE RECORD. HORACE HAS **2,746** STUFFED RATS IN HIS COLLECTION (1991). "I STUFFED THEM ALL BY MYSELF," HORACE TOLD US. "YOU SEE, BACK IN 1971 I TOOK A COURSE IN TAXIDERMY THROUGH THE MAIL AND I GUESSED THAT NO ONE ELSE WAS STUFFING RATS. I GUESS YOU MIGHT SAY THAT I BECAME ENGROSSED WITH STUFFING RATS." IT'S GROSS, HORACE, NOT ENGROSSED!

SWAMP SLIME (COLLECTION)

STUDENTS OF **MARSHVILLE HIGH SCHOOL**, BIG MARSH, FLORIDA, HOLD THE RECORD. DURING THEIR SUMMER VACATION IN 1991, THEY COLLECTED OVER **400 POUNDS** OF SWAMP SLIME. SINCE THEN, THE SLIME HAS BEEN ON DISPLAY ON THE SCHOOL'S AUDITORIUM STAGE. "WE'RE PROUD OF THE KIDS," DR. ANTHONY MARINO, THE SCHOOL'S PRINCIPAL, TOLD US. "THEY MADE GOOD USE OF THEIR SUMMER."

MUNCH
CHOMP
SLURP
XXX
FLOU

TAPEWORM
(LONGEST)

SALLY MAE WALLACE OF GREAT GRITS, MIS-
SISSIPPI, HOLDS THE RECORD. ON SEPTEMBER
5, 1991, DOCTORS EXTRACTED **37 FEET** (CONTIN-
UOUS) OF TAPEWORM FROM SALLY. "ABOUT AFTER
20 FEET OF THAT THING HAD COME OUT OF MY
MOUTH," SALLY TOLD US, "I JUST KNEW I HAD THE
RECORD. I WAS REALLY FILLED WITH JOY."

TARTAR (COLLECTION)

ALTHOUGH NO RECORDS HAVE BEEN KEPT, THE PEOPLE OF FISH FRY, LOUISIANA, SEEM THE LIKELY RECORD HOLDERS. FOR OVER A CENTURY, THEY HAVE BEEN COLLECTING TARTAR SCRAPED FROM THEIR TEETH. THEY COMBINE THE TARTAR WITH SOME SECRET INGREDIENTS AND SELL IT AS "FISH FRY'S ORIGINAL TARTAR SAUCE." IT'S GREAT ON FISH, WE WERE TOLD.

TEETH (X RAYS)

SALLY CARIES OF ATLANTA, GEORGIA, HOLDS THE RECORD. THE WALLS OF SALLY'S APARTMENT ARE PAPERED WITH TEETH X RAYS. THEY NUMBER WELL OVER **ONE MILLION** INDIVIDUAL PICTURES. "I'M PLEASED WITH THE RECORD," SALLY TOLD US, "BUT IT WASN'T ONE OF MY GOALS. I JUST WANTED THE APARTMENT TO LOOK PRETTY."

TOASTED FLY
(EATING)

TOM ALBERT, OF ITCHY PAWS, NEBRASKA, HOLDS THE RECORD. IN A CONTEST HELD ON MAY 30, 1988, TOM CONSUMED **2,500** TOASTED HOUSE FLIES IN LESS THAN FIVE MINUTES. HIS CLOSEST COMPETITOR DROPPED OUT, CLAIMING THAT SOMEONE HAD SLIPPED A HORSE FLY ON TO HIS PLATE. (**NOTE:** A LATER INSPECTION OF THE CONTENTS OF THE COMPETITOR'S STOMACH REVEALED NO HORSE FLY, AND THE JUDGES GAVE THE VICTORY AND THE RECORD TO TOM ALBERT.)

TOE JAM
⟨EATING⟩

SID BELLMORE OF MARMALADE DELLS, WIS-
CONSIN, HOLDS THIS DARING RECORD. ON
AUGUST 15, 1987, SID MANAGED TO GULP DOWN
THREE TEASPOONSFUL OF FRESH TOE JAM.
HIS CLOSEST COMPETITOR MANAGED TWO
TEASPOONSFUL, BUT THE SECOND WAS DIS-
ALLOWED BECAUSE THE CONTESTANT
COUGHED IT UP.

TOE JAM
(GROUP COLLECTION)

STUDENTS OF **GLORY WALK HIGH SCHOOL** IN GLORY WALK, PENNSYLVANIA, HOLD THE RECORD. IN 1991, THEY COLLECTED **14 GALLONS** OF TOE JAM. "I'M PLEASED," THE PRINCIPAL OF GLORY WALK HIGH TOLD US. "WE ENCOURAGE THE STUDENTS TO WORK TOGETHER, AND THIS RECORD CERTAINLY SHOWS THE VALUE OF TEAMWORK.

TOILET SEAT
(COLLECTION)

LOUIS CHARMIN, OF CHICAGO, ILLINOIS, HOLDS
THE RECORD. THROUGH 1992, LOUIS' TOILET
SEAT COLLECTION NUMBERED **1,153.** "I SUP-
POSE MY PRIZE SEAT IS AN IVORY ONE THAT
ONCE BELONGED TO ONE OF THE SHAHS OF
IRAN," LOUIS TOLD US, "BUT THEY'RE ALL IN-
TERESTING, AND EACH ONE, I SUPPOSE, HAS
A TALE TO TELL."

TONGUE (HAIRIEST)

SELMA RUBY, OF DALLAS, TEXAS, HOLDS
THE RECORD. SELMA'S TONGUE IS FULLY
COVERED WITH HAIR (1992). "I'VE BEEN
THINKING ABOUT HAVING IT REMOVED
BY AN ELECTROLYSIST," SELMA TOLD US,
"THOUGH LATELY PEOPLE HAVE BEEN
TELLING ME THAT IT'S BEAUTIFUL."

TRAIN PULL (WITH NOSTRILS)

WITH A HOOK SECURED TO HIS NOSTRILS, JEFF "STRONG NOSE" SADLER PULLED A STEAM ENGINE **100 YARDS** ALONG THE TRACKS AT HACKENSACK, NEW JERSEY, ON JUNE 12, 1991. THIS, TO OUR KNOWLEDGE, WAS THE ONLY SUCCESSFUL NOSTRIL PULL OF A TRAIN.

UNDERARM HAIR
(LENGTH)

FLORENCE FLOSS OF BAN, IDAHO, HOLDS THE RECORD. ON JULY 15, 1992, THE HAIR GROWING OUT OF FLORENCE'S LEFT ARMPIT STRETCHED TO A LENGTH OF 34 INCHES. THIS WAS MORE THAN ENOUGH FOR THE RECORD, BUT FLORENCE HOPES TO HAVE A YARD OF HAIR DANGLING FROM HER ARMPIT VERY SOON. "I SHAVE THE OTHER ARMPIT," FLORENCE REPORTED TO US.

VOMITING (IN SPACE)

YURI BARFNIKOV, A SOVIET COSMONAUT, HOLDS THE RECORD. WHILE WALKING ON THE MOON ON SEPTEMBER 13, 1987, YURI EXPERIENCED SOME STOMACH DISCOMFORT AND VOMITED. OFFICIALS FROM THE SOVIET UNION IMMEDIATELY CLAIMED THE RECORD, AND WHEN YURI RETURNED TO EARTH, HE WAS GIVEN A HERO'S WELCOME. (NOTE: IN A RARE GESTURE OF INTERNATIONAL COOPERATION, THE SOVIETS MADE THE TELEVISION FOOTAGE OF THIS AMAZING RECORD AVAILABLE FOR U.S. VIEWING.)

VOMITING
(TAPINGS)

AGNES ZENTER OF HILLSIDE, NEW JERSEY, HOLDS THE RECORD. THROUGH 1992, AGNES HAD CAPTURED ON TAPE 1,243 DIFFERENT PEOPLE IN THE ACT OF VOMITING. "I HATE VOMITING," AGNES TOLD US. "I ACTUALLY PREFER HEARING PEOPLE BLOW THEIR NOSES, BUT MY BROTHER BOB HAS TAPED SO MANY OF THEM THAT I HAD TO TRY FOR A DIFFERENT RECORD."

WATER BUG
⟨ EATING ⟩

CAPTAIN B. A. CRUNCH OF THE U.S. ARMY
HOLDS THE RECORD. IN A CONTEST HELD
ON APRIL 25, 1990, CAPTAIN CRUNCH ATE
4,321 WATER BUGS (COOKED IN A CORN POPPER)
IN A FOUR-HOUR SITTING. "I COULD HAVE EATEN
MORE," THE HAPPY OFFICER TOLD US, "BUT THE
JUDGES REFUSED TO ALLOW THEM TO BE
BUTTERED."

WISDOM TEETH (COLLECTION)

LINDA SAUNDERS, OF COLGATE, MISSOURI, HOLDS THE RECORD. THROUGH 1992, LINDA'S COLLECTION OF WISDOM TEETH NUMBERED 36,785. "IN A WAY MY MOTHER GOT ME STARTED," LINDA TOLD US. SHE SAVED ALL MY BABY TEETH, AND THAT INSPIRED ME." (NOTE: LINDA'S BABY TEETH ARE ON DISPLAY AT THE GROSSEST HALL OF RECORDS.)

EPILOGUE

Grossest Hall of Records

In 1990, plans were completed for the first permanent exhibit hall of gross memorabilia, and early in 1994 the hall will be opened to the public. Its site, the rear room of Lilly's Bar and Grill in downtown Swillington, Iowa, was selected from a list of thousands of applicants, and we believe it should attract millions of visitors annually.

At present, memorabilia collected for the permanent collection is being stored in a warehouse in Secaucus, New Jersey. The following description of items donated by record holders will probably send a chill up your spine. We certainly wish to extend our gratitude to the record holders, their families, and others for their generosity.

Memorabilia Donated

ADULT BODY (Baldest)—Adele Smith (Mrs. Ben Smith) donated a series of photos of Ben's bald body.

APPENDIX TRANSPLANT (From Hog)—Josef Podlawski provided the stuffed head of a hog that once owned his appendix.

ARMPIT (Sniffing)—Miriam Morton provided a complete list of all the people she has sniffed, including persons now deceased.

BELLY-BUTTON LINT (From The Stars)—Barry Barber donated a photo of his hand-vac.

BOOGER (Highest Priced)—Upshaw's, a New York City gallery, provided a wax impression of the highest-priced booger.

BOOGERS (From History)—Dr. Hans Friedlink donated a booger taken from the bullet-ridden body of John Dillinger.

BURPING (Group)—The mayor of Gassup, New Mexico, provided a cassette containing highlights from a burping recording.

CALLUS (Collection)—Florence Franklin donated a piece of callus autographed by Miklos Kometh, the rat-in-mouth marathon runner.

CAT TEETH (Collection)—Margie Norman donated fifty cat teeth taken from cats in each of fifty states.

CATERPILLAR-EATING (Live)—Walter Lucas provided a color photo of the green caterpillar that gave him the world's record.

CIGAR BUTTS (Collection)—Larry Lincoln donated a three-page autobiography covering most of the major events in his life.

COBWEBS (Eating)—Robert Armstrong donated an autographed first edition of his book, *Cutting Calories with Cobwebs.*

DANDRUFF (Eating)—The citizens of Gotshair provided 1,000 bags of "Honey Dandruff," their national candy.

DEAD BATS (Collection)—Dan Blake donated 13 dead bats for "good luck for the Grossest."

DEAD INSECTS (Collection)—Paul Roach donated 32,000 dead ants sealed in plastic and set as an outline map of New Hampshire.

DIET (Healthiest)—The people of Nature's Best provided a photo of their youngest resident eating his mother's lice.

EAR-WAX LICKING (From Pay Telephones)—Dan Dannon donated the "Let Dan Lick" plaque awarded to him by the Liberal Party of New York to protest the actions of the telephone company.

EYE GOOK (Collection)—Sandman Phillips provided an ounce of eye gook taken from a Tibetan Yak.

FEET (Smell)—Wanda Lake donated a pair of her shoes sealed for release in the event burglars should attempt to enter the Hall after hours.

GARBAGE (From The Stars)—Jack Keno donated a "mixed bag" from his world-famous Gag Bag shop.

GARLIC (Eating)—Joseph Van Dyke promised a week of his service as a "security guard."

HAIRIEST LEGS (Adult)—Rita Sims donated a lock of hair taken from her left ankle.

HEIGHT AND WEIGHT DIVINATION (Through Seat Analysis)—Subodh Rey provided a 15-minute videotape of his television quiz show, "You Bet Your Nose."

KISS OF DOG (Longest)—Evelyn Hunt donated an autographed copy of her book, *I Never Kissed a Collie.*

LEFTOVERS (Eating)—Lillian Bingham provided a list of "New York City's Top Spots for Leftovers" with tips on how to get them while they're still hot.

LONGEST BATH (Group)—The people of Culligan donated a railroad tank car filled with bath water "we used to set our fabulous record."

MUSCLES (Thigh)—Judy Burns provided a plaster cast of her leg "to be signed by the thousands of people who visit the Hall."

NOSE-STUFFING (Limburger Cheese)—Hans Kleiber donated the 13 ounces of Limburger cheese extracted from his nose on May 1, 1986.

NOSTRIL HAIR (Collection)—Alice Driston donated "the first nostril hair I ever tweezed. I took it from my grandmother. She was seriously ill, and I guess I just wanted something to remember her. She's gone, but now she'll never be forgotten."

PERSPIRATION (Collection)—The Sweet Sweat Bottling Company provided one dozen miniature bottles containing samples from the collection.

PLATE-LICKING—Gloria Evans donated a plate given to her by Kitchen Workers, Local 15, Chicago. It bears the inscription: "For Gloria: You've Licked Our Best and We Salute You."

POSTAGE STAMPS (Diet)—Herbert Winstead provided a copy of his best-selling book, *Stamping Out Fat.*

RAT TAILS (Collection)—Glenda Gabor donated a rat-tail rug for "your lobby." The attractive rug has a large, white "G" in its center area.

ROACH (Largest)—Rita Carson provided a color photo of herself and her pet roach leading the Rose Bowl Parade (1992) through downtown Pasadena.

SOCKS (Continuous Wear)—Andy Schwartz donated a photo of his bare feet taken in 1968.

SPITTING (Continuous)—The citizens of Down Wind provided a 12-minute film entitled "Highlights of the Annual Spitathon."

SPORT (Dead-Rat Throwing)—Dan Mann donated "the dead rat I tossed for the world's record."

SWAMP SLIME (Collection)—Dr. Anthony Marino provided a photo of the entire student body of Marshville High School taken "to provide inspiration for future generations of students."

TAPEWORM (Longest)—Sally Mae Wallace donated a videotape of her tryout for an appearance on "I've Got a Secret."

TOE JAM (Eating)—Sid Bellmore donated a copy of his wife's book, *The Secret on My Lips.*

TRAIN PULL (With Nostrils)—Jeff Sadler donated his nose. It was torn from his face in 1992 when he attempted to pull the Staten Island Ferry into its dock.

VOMITING (In Space)—Yuri Barfnikov's soiled helmet was donated by the Soviet Committee for Joint Space Cooperation.

WATER BUG (Eating)—The U.S. Army donated a recruiting poster of Captain Crunch.